51 ESSENTIAL CYBER TERMS EXPLAINED FOR LEADERS

A Non-Technical Guide. Each Term defined, Explained And With A Practical Example To Increase Your Leadership Impact

MARCO RYAN AND ANDREW FITZMAURICE

Pownall
Publishing

COPYRIGHT

CONTENTS

MARCO RYAN & ANDREW FITZMAURICE

INTRODUCTION

In today's rapidly evolving business world, with artificial intelligence challenging our core assumptions, the line between the physical and the cyber worlds blurs more with each passing day. Cybersecurity is no longer a siloed domain confined to IT departments; it has catapulted to the forefront of global attention, demanding the engagement of leaders across all sectors.

The infamous WannaCry ransomware attack of 2017, which affected over 200,000 computers across 150 countries, causing billions of dollars in damages, is a stark reminder of our collective vulnerability. This event underscored a critical truth: understanding cyber jargon is beneficial for tech professionals and imperative for leaders in every field.

As part of the Leadership Impact Series, this book, "51

Essential Cyber Terms Explained for Leaders" is designed to bridge the gap between the complex, often frightening world of cybersecurity and the strategic decision-making processes of leadership.

The goal is to demystify the labyrinth of cyber terminology, rendering it accessible and relevant to those who may be bewildered by the abbreviations or terms used by their IT colleagues. In doing so, this book aims to empower business leaders, enhancing their capacity to make informed decisions, communicate more effectively with technical teams, and, ultimately, bolster their organisation's cyber resilience.

Cybersecurity is a dynamic field, constantly adapting to new threats and technological advancements. As such, leaders cannot afford to be passive consumers of information; they must actively engage with the material, understanding not only what terms like "phishing," "malware," and "encryption" mean but also how they impact their operations and strategic planning.

Each term in this book is not merely defined but is accompanied by a jargon-free explanation that provides context to its importance in the broader landscape of digital security. Practical examples and case studies further illustrate how these concepts play out in real-world scenarios, providing readers with actionable insights they can apply within their organisations.

USING THE BOOK

The structure of this book is intentionally straightforward

and user-friendly. Terms are presented alphabetically, allowing for easy navigation and quick reference. Whether you're in a crucial meeting or strategising for the future, this book is designed to be your go-to resource for clarifying cyber concepts and jargon. By embracing the content, leaders will not only enhance their personal knowledge base but also contribute to fostering a culture of cyber awareness within their organisations—a critical step in safeguarding against the ever-evolving threats of the digital age.

But beyond just being able to find an answer about a specific term, mastering the language of cybersecurity is more than a strategic advantage; it's a necessity for future-proofing your career.

As digital transformation accelerates, leaders who are fluent in cyber issues command respect and credibility, not only within their teams but also in the broader business community. This proficiency opens new doors for professional growth and opportunities, positioning you as a forward-thinking leader prepared to exploit the opportunities of the 21st century.

The journey to cyber fluency may seem daunting, especially for those with a technical background. However, it's important to remember that the essence of leadership lies not in possessing all the answers but in asking the right questions and continually striving to learn. "51 Essential Cyber Terms Explained for Leaders" is more than a book; it's a tool for transformation designed to equip you with the knowledge and confidence needed to make a tangible impact in your organisation and beyond.

INCREASING YOUR IMPACT

In crafting this guide, we have drawn upon years of joint experience in the cyber domain, aiming to distil complex concepts into clear, concise explanations. We hope to help other leaders navigate the cyber landscape more efficiently and effectively by sharing this knowledge. The Leadership Impact Series embodies this ethos, offering a suite of resources tailored to demystify technical subjects and enhance leadership capabilities across a spectrum of disciplines.

As you continue gaining knowledge, we encourage you to approach each term with an open mind and a willingness to explore how it applies to your unique context. Cybersecurity is not static; it evolves in response to new threats and technologies. Likewise, your understanding of it should be dynamic, growing, and adapting as you apply these concepts to your leadership practice.

We invite you to view this book as a means to an end and a catalyst for broader change. By enhancing your cyber fluency, you're securing your organisation against digital threats and contributing to a more significant movement towards a more informed, resilient, and secure global community.

The path to leadership impact in the digital age begins here, with the foundational step of understanding the language of cybersecurity. Let's embark on this journey with the confidence that comes from knowing we're protecting our immediate interests and shaping a safer, more secure future for all.

Chapter One

FROM A TO C

APT (ADVANCED PERSISTENT THREAT)

DEFINITION

APT refers to a method where an unauthorized user gains access to a system or network and remains undetected for an extended period. The purpose is usually to steal data rather than cause damage, characterized by their sophistication and persistence.

APT EXPLAINED

In the shadows of cyberspace, a digital specter lurks – the Advanced Persistent Threat (APT). This isn't your everyday cyber attack; it's a slow, methodical siege. Like a spy infiltrating an organization, APTs slip through the cracks, undetected, sometimes for years. Their mission? To gather intelligence, steal secrets, or monitor activities. They're the ultimate undercover agents of the cyber world, using advanced techniques, patience, and stealth. APTs target high-value entities – governments, corporations, and critical infrastructures – making them a formidable challenge for even the most robust security defenses.

AN APT EXAMPLE

Few events have echoed as ominously in the digital theatre of war as the SolarWinds hack of 2020. An epitome of an Advanced Persistent Threat, this saga unfolded stealthily, with the precision of a mastermind. The attackers believed to be backed by a nation-state, cunningly implanted malicious code into SolarWinds' Orion software, used extensively by government agencies and Fortune 500 companies.

The breach was not just an attack but a statement – a chilling demonstration of vulnerability at the highest echelons. Sensitive data became the spoils of this digital heist, leading to a tense geopolitical standoff. The SolarWinds incident was more than a security breach; it was a wake-up call, a reminder of the ever-present digital shadow cast by APTs, ready to engulf the unwary in its silent, menacing embrace.

BOTNET

DEFINITION

A botnet is a network of devices infected with malicious software controlled remotely by a hacker, typically without the device owners' knowledge. Botnets are usually deployed to send spam emails or carry out DDoS attacks.

BOTNET EXPLAINED

Imagine a puppet master with a vast array of strings, each connected to a device – computers, smartphones, even IoT gadgets. This is the unsettling reality of botnets. They turn everyday devices into soldiers in an army of the unwilling, controlled by a remote attacker. These devices then execute coordinated tasks – sending spam, launching denial-of-service attacks, or spreading malware. The individual devices might show no signs of compromise, functioning normally while secretly contributing to the botnet's collective power. This covert mobilization makes botnets a formidable weapon in the cyber criminal's arsenal.

A BOTNET EXAMPLE

In the autumn of 2016, the cyber world witnessed an unprecedented siege – the Mirai botnet attack. Its weapon of choice? Innumerable everyday IoT devices, from cameras to routers, have infected and transformed into a relentless digital army. The attack targeted Dyn, a key DNS provider, resulting in widespread outages across significant sites like Twitter and Netflix.

But Mirai's tale was not just about the chaos it unleashed. It was a narrative that shook the core of Internet security, revealing how the innocuous devices populating our homes could become disruptive instruments. The aftermath was a period of reckoning as the Internet community grappled with the vulnerabilities exposed and the lessons painfully learned. Mirai was not just an attack; it was a precursor, a stark reminder of the fragility of our interconnected digital existence.

BYOD (BRING YOUR OWN DEVICE)

DEFINITION

BYOD is a policy allowing employees to use their personal devices, such as smartphones, laptops, or tablets, for work purposes. It aims to increase productivity and flexibility but also introduces various security challenges.

BYOD EXPLAINED

Imagine a workplace where your personal phone or laptop doubles as your work device, blending the personal and professional. This is BYOD, a concept that reflects the modern work-life fusion. Employees enjoy the convenience and comfort of their own devices, potentially boosting morale and productivity. However, it's not without risks. Personal devices may lack the stringent security measures of company-provided equipment, making them potential gateways for security breaches. Companies embracing BYOD must balance flexibility with robust security policies to protect corporate data.

A BYOD EXAMPLE

In 2023, an innovative tech startup in Silicon Valley embraced BYOD, reflecting its culture of flexibility and empowerment. However, the company understood the risks and implemented a comprehensive BYOD policy. It required secure VPN connections, enforced regular security updates, and provided cybersecurity training for employees.

This proactive approach paid off when an employee's device was lost. Thanks to the stringent security measures and remote wipe capabilities, the company swiftly secured the device's data, preventing potential data leakage. The incident highlighted the effectiveness of the company's BYOD strategy, marrying convenience with security and setting an example for others in the industry to follow.

CISO (CHIEF INFORMATION SECURITY OFFICER)

DEFINITION

The CISO is a senior-level executive responsible for an organization's information and data security. While the role varies across organizations, it typically involves overseeing the overall IT security strategy, managing security technologies, and responding to incidents.

CISO EXPLAINED

Imagine a general on the battlefield of cybersecurity, overseeing the defense of an organization's most valuable digital assets. This is the role of a CISO. With cyber threats growing more sophisticated, the CISO is the strategic leader who navigates the complex landscape of digital security. They are not just defenders but visionaries, shaping the cybersecurity strategy, ensuring compliance with regulations, and fostering a culture of security awareness throughout the organization. In an age where data breaches can make or break companies, the CISO is a pivotal figure, orchestrating the collective effort to safeguard digital fortresses.

A CISO EXAMPLE

In 2023, a major European bank appointed a seasoned cyber intelligence expert as its new CISO amidst rising cyber threats in the financial sector. The new CISO spearheaded a transformative security overhaul, integrating advanced AI-driven threat detection systems and championing a bank-wide cybersecurity awareness program.

This strategic shift quickly bore fruit when the bank successfully thwarted a sophisticated cyber attack targeting its transaction systems. The incident was a victory against a potential breach, validating the CISO's foresight and leadership in steering the bank towards a robust, proactive cybersecurity posture.

CSRF (CROSS-SITE REQUEST FORGERY)

ITS DEFINITION

CSRF is an attack that forces unwanted actions on a web application to happen by the end-user when they're authenticated. Attackers exploit the trust a web application has in the user's browser.

CSRF EXPLAINED

Imagine a marionette unwittingly controlled by a hidden puppeteer. CSRF operates similarly, turning an innocent user's browser into a puppet that performs actions without the user's knowledge. When logged into a website, CSRF can manipulate your browser to send unauthorized commands to the website, exploiting the trust it has in your authenticated session. These attacks can result in unintended fund transfers, changed passwords, or compromised personal data. The insidious nature of CSRF lies in its deception, manipulating users and websites to breach the sanctity of digital interactions.

A CSRF EXAMPLE

The tale of betrayal in cyberspace found a stark embodiment in the CSRF attack against a popular social media platform in 2019. Trapped by the deceptive scheme, users found their settings altered, their posts modified, and their private messages sent without consent. The platform, revered for its connectivity, became an unwitting accomplice in the attack, processing the forged requests as legitimate.

The aftermath was a storm of outrage and a hard-earned lesson in digital trust. The platform, once a bastion of communication, had to fortify its defenses, ensuring that the trust placed in it by millions was not misplaced. The CSRF attack was not just a breach; it was a poignant narrative about the fragile nature of trust in the digital age and the perils that lurk when that trust is subverted.

.

MARCO RYAN & ANDREW FITZMAURICE

Chapter Two

FROM D TO E

DDOS (DISTRIBUTED DENIAL OF SERVICE)

DEFINITION

Distributed Denial of Service Attack: often used by hackers to overwhelm websites with traffic and bring them grinding to a halt, disrupting normal service. This is where multiple DoS Attacks are launched from more than one location. Botnets are often used in this kind of attack.

DDOS EXPLAINED

A DDoS attack is the digital equivalent of a mob crowding a store, making it impossible for legitimate customers to enter. In this cyber onslaught, many compromised devices, often part of a botnet, flood a target server with traffic. This deluge of data requests overwhelms the server, causing slowdowns or complete shutdowns. The danger of DDoS lies in its ability to disrupt services and camouflage more insidious attacks amidst the chaos.

A DDOS EXAMPLE

In a defining moment of 2021, a prominent online gaming service became the arena for a colossal DDoS confrontation. As millions of gamers settled in for an evening of entertainment, the hackers released an invisible digital torrent. The service, a titan in the gaming world, staggered under the relentless barrage, its servers besieged by a flood of bogus traffic.

But this was no mere disruption; it was a meticulously orchestrated attack, aiming to cripple the service and tarnish its reputation. The gaming giant, rallying its defenses, managed to mitigate the assault, ensuring the continuity of its services against overwhelming odds.

The incident was not just a battle against digital disruption but a stark testament to the resilience required in the face of the ever-evolving cyber threats. It underscored the importance of vigilance and preparedness in an era where the battleground is as digital as it is physical and where every data byte can be a weapon or a shield.

DKIM (DOMAIN KEYS IDENTIFIED MAIL)

DEFINITION

DKIM is an email authentication method designed to detect email spoofing. It allows the sender to attach a digital signature to emails, which receiving email servers can use to verify that the email was sent from the legitimate domain it claims to be from and that its contents have not been tampered with.

DKIM EXPLAINED

Imagine sending a sealed letter with a unique stamp that assures the recipient it's genuinely from you and hasn't been tampered with. DKIM does this for emails. It attaches a digital signature to outgoing messages, verifying the sender's domain and ensuring the content remains unchanged in transit. In an era where email spoofing and phishing are rampant, DKIM acts as a guardian of email authenticity, helping to maintain trust in digital communication by assuring recipients that their emails are legitimate and secure.

A DKIM EXAMPLE

In 2023, a global non-profit organization faced a surge in phishing attacks. Attackers spoofed the organization's email domain to solicit donations fraudulently. By implementing DKIM, the organization fortified its email security, enabling email servers worldwide to verify the authenticity of emails originating from its domain.

The impact was immediate and profound. The fraudulent emails were swiftly flagged and filtered, restoring the integrity of communications from the non-profit. The successful deployment of DKIM turned a period of vulnerability into a milestone in digital trust, underscoring the critical role of email authentication in the fight against cyber deception.

DMZ (DEMILITARIZED ZONE)

DEFINITION

In cybersecurity, a DMZ is a subnetwork that separates an internal local area network (LAN) from external networks, typically the Internet. It's a buffer zone where external-facing services (like web and email servers) are placed, adding an extra layer of security.

DMZ EXPLAINED

Imagine a castle with an outer courtyard. This courtyard is a buffer, protecting the inner sanctum from direct attack. In the digital realm, the DMZ is that courtyard. It's where organizations place services that need to be accessible from the outside world, like web servers, while keeping the rest of the internal network more secure. The DMZ acts as a buffer, allowing organizations to control and monitor access, reducing the risk of external attacks reaching the critical parts of their network.

A DMZ EXAMPLE

In 2023, a large US hospital group restructured its network architecture, establishing a robust DMZ as part of its enhanced cybersecurity framework. This strategic move came just in time. Later that year, a wave of cyber attacks targeted healthcare providers.

The hospital's DMZ effectively isolated the attack, preventing it from penetrating deeper into the network. Thanks to the foresight and strategic planning of the hospital's IT team, critical patient data and internal systems remained secure.

The DMZ served as a digital moat and a testament to the hospital's commitment to patient privacy and data security.

DPI (DEEP PACKET INSPECTION)

DEFINITION

DPI is an advanced network packet filtering method that examines the packet's data part (and possibly the header) as it passes an inspection point. It monitors, detects, and blocks malicious or unwanted traffic based on content rather than just by IP or port.

DPI EXPLAINED

Imagine a security checkpoint scrutinizing your ID, ticket, and luggage contents. DPI does this for network traffic. It dives deep into the data packets traveling through a network, examining their content to identify, manage, or block packets that pose a security threat or violate policies. DPI is like a discerning gatekeeper, ensuring that only safe, compliant traffic flows through while potentially harmful data is stopped in its tracks.

A DPI EXAMPLE

In 2023, a leading European ISP implemented DPI across its network to enhance its security and service quality. The move was visionary, especially when a sophisticated new malware strain began spreading through seemingly innocuous network traffic.

With DPI, the ISP could detect and neutralize the malware in real-time, safeguarding its infrastructure and millions of subscribers from potential harm. The ISP's proactive approach, leveraging DPI's granular inspection capabilities, set a new standard in network security and management, demonstrating the power of deep insight in maintaining the integrity and safety of digital communications.

EDR (ENDPOINT DETECTION AND RESPONSE)

DEFINITION

EDR is a cybersecurity solution that monitors endpoint devices (such as computers and mobile devices) to detect and respond to cyber threats. It collects and analyses data to identify suspicious activities, enabling quick response to mitigate attacks.

EDR EXPLAINED

Imagine a security system in your home that not only alerts you to intruders but also tracks their movements, learns their tactics, and helps you stop them in their tracks. EDR does this for network endpoints. It's like having a highly trained security guard for each device, constantly vigilant for signs of compromise. By analyzing behaviors and patterns, EDR can spot anomalies that might indicate a cyber attack, often before significant damage is done. It's a critical line of defense in today's landscape, where endpoints are frequently the target of sophisticated attacks.

AN EDR EXAMPLE

In 2022, a multinational corporation faced a sophisticated cyber espionage campaign aimed at stealing intellectual property. The attackers used previously unknown malware that bypassed traditional antivirus solutions. However, the company's EDR system flagged unusual data exfiltration attempts from several endpoints.

Thanks to the EDR's detailed forensic data, the security team quickly isolated the affected machines and identified the malware's unique characteristics. This swift response stopped the data breach and provided valuable intelligence for preventing future incidents. The event underscored the indispensable role of EDR in modern cybersecurity strategies, highlighting its effectiveness in identifying and mitigating threats beyond the reach of conventional defenses.

ENCRYPTION

DEFINITION

Encryption converts data or information into a code to prevent unauthorized access. It's critical for protecting data privacy in various digital communications and transactions.

ENCRYPTION EXPLAINED

Imagine you have a secret diary you want to keep away from prying eyes. Encryption is like an indecipherable code that locks away your words, making them accessible only to those with the key. Encryption ensures that sensitive information – emails, online transactions, or personal data – remains secure and unreadable to unauthorized entities. Whether safeguarding against eavesdroppers or protecting data integrity, encryption is the silent sentinel, guarding the confidentiality of our digital interactions.

AN ENCRYPTION EXAMPLE

In a groundbreaking event of 2022, a renowned global bank unveiled a cutting-edge encrypted messaging platform. This platform was not just a tool for secure communication; it was a fortress designed to shield the confidential conversations of high-profile clients from the relentless threats of cyber espionage.

The initiative was born from a saga of relentless cyber attacks targeting the financial sector, where information is the most coveted asset. The bank, recognizing the urgency of the threat, embarked on a mission to redefine the paradigm of secure communication.

As the platform went live, it marked a new era of digital confidentiality. The encrypted messages traversed cyberspace like armored convoys, impervious to the lurking predators of the digital deep. Once a target, the bank had transformed into a beacon of security, setting a new standard for privacy and trust in an industry where the stakes are always high and the secrets are worth fortunes.

The narrative of the encrypted messaging platform was more than a technological triumph; it was a testament to the indomitable spirit of innovation, a reminder that in the face of adversity, the quest for security and privacy is an ever-evolving journey.

Chapter Three

FROM F TO H

FIREWALL

DEFINITION

As its name suggests, a firewall acts as a barrier between networks or parts of a network, blocking malicious traffic or preventing hacking attempts. A network firewall is installed on the boundary between two networks. This is usually located between the Internet and an organisation's network. It can be a piece of hardware or software running on a computer that acts as a gateway to the company network. A client firewall is software that runs on an end user's computer, protecting only that computer. In either case, the firewall inspects all traffic, both inbound and outbound, to see if it meets certain criteria (rules). If it does, it is allowed; if not, the firewall blocks it.

FIREWALL EXPLAINED

Picture a fortress with a vigilant gatekeeper scrutinising every visitor and selectively deciding who may enter and who must be turned away. This is the essence of a firewall in the digital domain. It serves as a digital gatekeeper for your network, meticulously examining data packets that seek entry or exit. Firewalls enforce security policies, deciding whether to block or allow traffic based on predetermined rules. They stand guard at the boundaries of your digital domain, shielding it from the myriad threats lurking in the vast wilderness of the Internet.

A FIREWALL EXAMPLE

In late 2022, a renowned US healthcare provider faced an alarming surge in cyber attack attempts. Their network, a repository of sensitive patient data, was a prime target for cybercriminals. The organisation's salvation came in the form of an advanced firewall system.

This firewall wasn't just a barrier but an intelligent guardian equipped with the latest threat detection and response capabilities. When a particularly sophisticated attack threatened to breach the network, the firewall's advanced algorithms sprang into action. It analysed the attack patterns, blocked the intrusion attempt, and alerted the IT team in real time.

This incident was more than a thwarted attack; it validated the healthcare provider's foresight in fortifying its digital defences. Once a silent sentinel, the firewall emerged as the unsung hero, ensuring the integrity of critical healthcare data and the trust of countless patients and providers.

FIM (FILE INTEGRITY MONITORING)

DEFINITION

FIM is a security process that monitors and alerts on unauthorised changes to critical system files, directories, and configurations. It's essential for detecting potential security breaches or compliance violations by ensuring that critical files remain unaltered by unauthorised users.

FIM EXPLAINED

Imagine having a meticulous librarian who keeps track of every book in the library, noticing if a book is misplaced, altered, or taken without permission. FIM acts like this librarian for your computer systems, vigilantly monitoring files to ensure they haven't been tampered with. Whether due to malicious activity, such as malware infection or user unauthorised changes, FIM helps identify anomalies that could signal a compromise. It's a crucial tool for maintaining the integrity of systems and ensuring compliance with stringent regulatory standards.

A FIM EXAMPLE

In 2023, a government agency responsible for sensitive public records implemented a state-of-the-art FIM solution to enhance its cybersecurity posture. This move proved invaluable when an insider attempted to modify critical data files undetected.

The FIM system immediately alerted the IT security team to the unauthorised changes, allowing them to investigate and reverse them quickly. The incident prevented potential data manipulation and highlighted the significance of FIM in safeguarding against insider threats. This proactive approach demonstrated the agency's commitment to data integrity and transparency, reinforcing public trust in protecting sensitive information.

GDPR (GENERAL DATA PROTECTION REGULATION)

DEFINITION

GDPR is a data privacy and protection regulation in EU law that covers the European Union and the European Economic Area. It also covers the transfer of personal data outside the EU and EEA.

GDPR EXPLAINED

In an era where personal data is as valuable as currency, the GDPR is a beacon of rights and respect. It's a comprehensive set of rules designed to empower individuals, giving them control over their personal data while imposing strict obligations on those who process it. Companies must ensure transparency, secure consent, and provide rights for individuals to access, rectify, or erase their data. GDPR reshaped the digital landscape, making data privacy a fundamental right rather than an afterthought.

A GDPR EXAMPLE

In 2021, the GDPR made headlines when the Irish Data Protection Commission levied a monumental fine of €225 million against WhatsApp. The issue was transparency – or the lack thereof – about how WhatsApp shared user data with its parent company, Facebook.

This case was a stark reminder of the new era ushered in by GDPR. It signified that the veil of ambiguity around data practices would no longer be tolerated. Companies worldwide were put on notice to respect user privacy, provide clear information, or face the formidable force of GDPR's financial penalties.

GRC (GOVERNANCE, RISK MANAGEMENT, AND COMPLIANCE)

DEFINITION

GRC is an integrated framework for managing an organisation's overall governance, risk management strategies, and compliance with regulations. It helps organisations ensure they operate ethically, within legal parameters, and effectively manage risks.

GRC EXPLAINED

Think of GRC as the compass, map, and rules for navigating a ship through treacherous waters. Governance steers the organisation, ensuring decisions align with strategic goals. Risk management is the map, identifying potential hazards and plotting a safe course. Compliance is the rulebook, keeping the journey within legal and ethical bounds. Together, they form a cohesive strategy that enables organisations to operate smoothly, minimise risks, and comply with laws and standards. GRC is about creating a culture where doing the right thing for the right reason is part of the organisational DNA.

A GRC EXAMPLE

In 2020, a global pharmaceutical company faced significant challenges with evolving healthcare regulations and heightened scrutiny over data privacy practices. By adopting a robust GRC framework, the company could streamline its compliance processes, effectively manage risks associated with clinical trials, and uphold the highest governance standards.

This strategic approach facilitated compliance with complex international regulations and fostered a culture of integrity and transparency. As a result, the company safeguarded its reputation and positioned itself as an industry leader in ethical practices. The success story became a benchmark, illustrating the critical role of GRC in navigating the complex regulatory landscape of the pharmaceutical industry.

HONEYPOT

DEFINITION

A honeypot is a security mechanism that detects, deflects, or studies attempts at unauthorised use of information systems. It's designed to mimic systems that an intruder would like to break into but isolates and monitors them. It is also used to describe state or serious organized crime activities where human interactions are used to illicit proprietary/damaging information from a human target to the benefit of those with a hostile intent.

HONEYPOT EXPLAINED

Envision a decoy, a trap so convincingly real that it lures in the most cautious predators. This is the principle behind a honeypot in cybersecurity. It's a deliberately vulnerable system, a digital mirage designed to attract attackers. Once they take the bait, their methods, tactics, and tools are observed and logged. Honeypots are the cyber equivalent of undercover surveillance, providing invaluable intelligence on enemy tactics and bolstering real systems' defences by learning from these interactions.

A HONEYPOT EXAMPLE

In 2023, a significant European bank unveiled a groundbreaking defence strategy against cyber threats: an elaborate network of honeypots disguised as vulnerable points in the bank's digital infrastructure. This clever ruse was not merely a trap but a sophisticated intelligence-gathering operation.

As attackers, drawn by the allure of apparent vulnerabilities, infiltrated these honeypots, their every move was monitored, analysed, and counteracted. This strategy turned the tables on the attackers, transforming potential breaches into a rich source of insights, fortifying the bank's real defences, and staying one step ahead of the cybercriminal underworld.

This initiative marked a transformative approach to cybersecurity, where deception becomes a powerful tool in the digital arsenal, turning potential threats into opportunities for reinforcement and resilience.

MARCO RYAN & ANDREW FITZMAURICE

Chapter Four

FROM I TO YET MORE I

ICS (INDUSTRIAL CONTROL SYSTEMS)

DEFINITION

ICS are integrated hardware and software designed to control and monitor industrial processes, such as manufacturing, power generation, and water treatment. They are critical to ensuring the smooth operation of industrial infrastructures but can be vulnerable to cyber threats.

ICS EXPLAINED

Think of ICS as the central nervous system of a factory or power plant, controlling everything from assembly lines to electricity flow. These systems ensure that processes run efficiently, safely, and reliably. However, as they become more interconnected with IT networks and the Internet, they also become cyber attack targets. Protecting these systems is about safeguarding data and ensuring facilities' and communities' physical safety. The cybersecurity of ICS is a vital aspect of national security and public safety in our increasingly automated and connected world.

AN ICS EXAMPLE

In 2019, a European energy provider faced a sophisticated cyber attack aimed at its ICS. The attackers attempted to disrupt power distribution, potentially causing widespread outages. However, the company's investment in advanced cybersecurity measures for its ICS, including real-time monitoring and anomaly detection, allowed it to quickly identify and isolate the attack.

The swift response prevented any disruption to the power supply, showcasing the importance of securing ICS in critical infrastructure sectors. The incident served as a wake-up call for industries worldwide, emphasising the need for robust cybersecurity defences in an era where cyber-attacks can have tangible, potentially catastrophic, real-world consequences.

IDAM (IDENTITY AND ACCESS MANAGEMENT)

DEFINITION

IDAM systems provide tools and technologies for assigning different access rights to critical information for users within an organisation. They permit trusted individuals to access the correct resources at the right times for legitimate reasons.

IDAM EXPLAINED

Imagine a high-security facility where every door opens only for the right person, at the right time, under the right conditions. IDAM makes this precision possible in the digital realm. It's a framework that ensures users are genuinely who they claim to be and have appropriate access to company resources. Whether logging into a system, accessing confidential data, or performing critical operations, IDAM verifies and validates every action, keeping unauthorised intruders at bay and ensuring that the right individuals are afforded the correct privileges.

AN IDAM EXAMPLE

In mid-2023, a leading global technology firm faced a critical challenge. Ensuring secure and efficient access was paramount, with a workforce spanning continents and countless digital assets to manage. The company deployed a state-of-the-art IDAM solution, transforming its security landscape.

This IDAM system wasn't just a gatekeeper but a dynamic business enabler. It ensured employees could access the needed resources seamlessly while maintaining stringent security protocols. When an attempt was made to access sensitive data outside of normal parameters, the IDAM system promptly intervened, preventing potential data breaches.

The success of this IDAM implementation was a testament to the company's commitment to security and efficiency. It showcased the pivotal role of IDAM in safeguarding assets while empowering a global workforce in today's interconnected business environment.

IDS (INTRUSION DETECTION SYSTEM)

DEFINITION

An IDS is a device or software application designed to monitor network or system activities for malicious activities or policy violations and report them to a management station.

IDS EXPLAINED

Imagine a high-tech surveillance system in a top-secret facility, constantly scanning for unauthorised access or suspicious movements. An IDS functions similarly within a network, acting as the digital eyes and ears of an organisation's cybersecurity team. It meticulously analyses network traffic and system activities, searching for signs of intrusion, such as known malware signatures or unusual data patterns. When something fishy is detected, the IDS raises the alarm, alerting administrators to potential threats. While it doesn't prevent intrusions, its early warnings can mitigate damage and fortify defences.

AN IDS EXAMPLE

In the spring of 2021, a prominent online retailer experienced an attempted breach. The attackers aimed to infiltrate the network and steal customer data. However, the company's IDS, equipped with the latest threat intelligence, quickly detected unusual traffic patterns indicating a potential attack.

The security team was alerted in real-time, enabling them to swiftly investigate and block the attack vectors the intruders were attempting to exploit. This rapid response prevented data compromise and maintained the integrity of the retailer's operations. The incident highlighted the indispensable role of IDS in the cybersecurity ecosystem, offering a critical layer of insight and defence against ever-evolving cyber threats.

IOT (INTERNET OF THINGS)

DEFINITION

IoT refers to the worldwide collection of physical objects—" things"—that contain embedded sensors, software, and other emerging technologies that can connect and exchange data with other devices and systems connected via the Internet.

IOT EXPLAINED

Picture a world where your fridge can order milk before you run out, your thermostat adjusts the temperature based on your preferences, and your car warns you about upcoming maintenance—all without human intervention. This is the Internet of Things (IoT). It's a network of devices, from everyday household items to sophisticated industrial tools, all interconnected and communicating. These devices collect and share data, making everything more connected, efficient, and smart. However, this connectivity also opens up new vulnerabilities, making security a paramount concern in the IoT universe.

AN IOT EXAMPLE

In a bustling smart city project in 2022, a European municipality embarked on an ambitious journey to integrate IoT across public services. Streetlights adjusted brightness based on foot traffic, waste bins notified collection services when full, and public transport optimised routes in real-time. However, this interconnected utopia faced its baptism by fire—a coordinated cyber-attack targeting the city's IoT infrastructure.

The attack was designed to disrupt, turning smart devices into pawns of chaos. But the city was prepared. A robust IoT security framework, including real-time monitoring and AI-driven anomaly detection, swiftly identified and isolated the compromised devices, averting a potential crisis.

This incident wasn't just a close call but a testament to the city's foresight in embedding security into the fabric of its IoT landscape. It highlighted the double-edged nature of our interconnected world, where the threads connecting and enriching our lives can also become vectors of vulnerability.

Chapter Five

FROM I TO K

IPS (INTRUSION PREVENTION SYSTEM)

DEFINITION

An IPS is a network security/threat prevention technology that examines network traffic flows to detect and prevent vulnerability exploits. Unlike an IDS, which only detects and alerts, an IPS also takes corrective action to block potential threats.

IPS EXPLAINED

Building on the previous analogy, if an IDS is like a surveillance system alerting you to intruders, then an IPS is akin to having security guards who not only detect intruders but also take immediate action to stop them in their tracks. It actively analyses network data, looks for malicious activities or policy breaches, and can automatically block harmful traffic or activities before they inflict damage. An IPS is a proactive defense in the cybersecurity arsenal, providing a crucial barrier against attacks that bypass traditional security measures.

AN IPS EXAMPLE

In late 2022, a government agency's network came under a sophisticated cyberattack aimed at disrupting public services. The attackers deployed a new strain of malware designed to evade detection. However, the agency's IPS, armed with advanced behavioral analysis capabilities, identified and blocked the malicious traffic in real-time, preventing the malware from reaching its targets.

This proactive defense ensured the continuity of essential services and safeguarded sensitive data against compromise. The IPS's effectiveness in thwarting the attack reaffirmed the value of having an active and adaptive security layer capable of responding to threats as they emerge.

IR (INCIDENT RESPONSE)

DEFINITION

IR is a structured methodology for handling security breaches or cyberattacks, including identifying, containing, eradicating, and recovering from incidents to minimize their impact and prevent future occurrences. It covers not only a single organisation, but must be coherent with an organisations ecosystem of stakeholders and suppliers.

IR EXPLAINED

Imagine a well-drilled emergency response team springing into action at the first sign of a fire. They have plans, tools, and protocols ready to contain the damage and restore safety. IR operates under a similar premise in cybersecurity. It's a comprehensive approach that kicks in when a security breach is detected, employing a series of strategic steps to quickly contain the threat, eliminate it, and recover normal operations. Moreover, it involves analyzing the incident to bolster defenses against future attacks, turning each challenge into a learning opportunity.

AN IR EXAMPLE

In early 2022, a leading software development firm fell victim to a ransomware attack that encrypted critical project data. Thanks to a well-prepared IR plan, the company responded decisively. They isolated the affected systems to prevent the spread of ransomware, used backups to restore encrypted data, and applied patches to close the security gaps exploited by the attackers.

The firm's swift and effective response minimized operational downtime and protected its reputation. Post-incident analysis led to enhanced security measures, demonstrating the IR's role in crisis management and driving continuous improvement in cybersecurity practices.

ISMS (INFORMATION SECURITY MANAGEMENT SYSTEM)

DEFINITION

An ISMS is a systematic approach to managing sensitive company information so that it remains secure. It includes people, processes, and IT systems by applying a risk management process.

ISMS EXPLAINED

Consider ISMS as the master plan for safeguarding an organization's information assets. It's not just about deploying the latest security technologies but creating a comprehensive framework that encompasses policies, procedures, and controls tailored to manage and mitigate risks to information security. An ISMS considers the diverse ways information is processed, stored, and accessed, ensuring a holistic defense strategy that aligns with the organization's objectives and regulatory requirements. It's about embedding security into the organization's very fabric, creating a culture where information protection is a shared responsibility.

AN ISMS EXAMPLE

A multinational corporation, facing growing threats to its intellectual property and customer data, implemented an ISMS to strengthen its information security posture. This strategic move involved a thorough risk assessment, resulting in robust security policies, employee training programs, and enhanced physical and digital controls.

Within a year, the corporation achieved compliance with

international standards such as ISO/IEC 27001 and significantly reduced data breaches and leak incidents. This transformation underscored the effectiveness of ISMS in fostering a secure and resilient organizational environment capable of adapting to the evolving cybersecurity landscape.

ISO (INTERNATIONAL ORGANISATION FOR STANDARDISATION)

DEFINITION

ISO is an independent, non-governmental international organization developing standards to ensure product, service, system quality, safety, and efficiency. In cybersecurity, ISO standards like ISO/IEC 27001 provide criteria for information security management systems.

ISO EXPLAINED

Imagine a world where every product, service, or system adheres to universally recognized quality and reliability benchmarks. That's the vision ISO strives to achieve. In cybersecurity, ISO standards are a blueprint for organizations to establish, implement, maintain, and continuously improve their information security management. Adhering to these standards enhances security practices and builds trust with customers, partners, and regulators by demonstrating a commitment to safeguarding information assets.

AN ISO EXAMPLE

In 2023, a global financial institution sought to bolster customer confidence amidst growing data privacy and security concerns.

By adopting the ISO/IEC 27001 standard, the institution began a rigorous process to revamp its cybersecurity measures, aligning them with international best practices.

The certification process was demanding, requiring a comprehensive audit of the institution's information security management system. However, achieving ISO certification marked a significant milestone, publicly affirming the institution's dedication to the highest information security standards. This commitment reinforced customer trust and set a competitive benchmark in the finance industry, showcasing the pivotal role of ISO standards in advancing cybersecurity excellence.

KEYLOGGER

DEFINITION

A keylogger is a type of surveillance technology used to record and store keystrokes typed by a user. IT organizations often use Keyloggers to troubleshoot technical problems with computers and business networks. Still, they can be used maliciously to steal information.

KEYLOGGER EXPLAINED

Imagine someone discreetly noting everything you write, from private messages to passwords. That's what a keylogger does digitally. It's a stealthy tool that records every keystroke on a computer, capturing everything typed by the user. While keyloggers can be used legitimately for monitoring or troubleshooting, they are also a favored tool in the cybercriminal's arsenal, often used to steal sensitive information such as login credentials, credit card numbers, and personal messages. The insidious power of keyloggers lies in their silence; users usually don't know they're being watched, making them a potent threat in the digital world.

A KEYLOGGER EXAMPLE

In a high-profile corporate espionage case in 2023, a leading tech company in the United States discovered a keylogger embedded in its system. The device was not just recording keystrokes; it was a portal into the company's most guarded secrets.

The keylogger had been clandestinely installed on a top executive's computer, capturing every keystroke, password, and confidential email. But the breach was more than an intrusion; it was a calculated strike at the heart of the company's strategic plans.

The revelation sent shockwaves through the corporate world. The company, acting swiftly, tightened its security protocols, reinforcing its digital fortress. This incident was a stark reminder of the relentless threat landscape and the constant vigilance required to safeguard the sanctity of digital information.

MARCO RYAN & ANDREW FITZMAURICE

Chapter Six

FROM M TO N

MALWARE

DEFINITION

Malware, sometimes called malicious software, is any program or file harmful to a computer user. Types of malware include viruses, worms, Trojan horses, spyware and ransomware.

MALWARE EXPLAINED

Malware is the catch-all term for the digital equivalent of pathogens. As viruses and bacteria can wreak havoc on the human body, malware can infect and damage computers, steal data, or hijack resources. It comes in many forms, each with its modus operandi—viruses that spread and corrupt, worms that replicate across networks, Trojans that disguise themselves as harmless software, and ransomware that holds data hostage. The proliferation of malware is a constant battle in the digital world, requiring vigilant defence and proactive countermeasures to protect against these pervasive digital threats.

A MALWARE EXAMPLE

In the spring of 2023, a large retail chain in the UK faced the nightmare scenario every business dreads — a widespread malware attack. The malware, a sophisticated ransomware strain, encrypted the company's critical data, grinding operations to a halt and demanding a hefty ransom for the decryption key.

The attack was more than a disruption; it was a siege, holding the company's digital assets hostage and threatening its reputation. However, the retail giant was not one to bow to cyber extortion. With a robust backup and disaster recovery strategy, the company restored its systems, refusing to negotiate with the attackers.

This incident was not just a tale of resilience and recovery; it was a sobering reminder of the ever-present threat of malware and the paramount importance of preparedness and resilience in the face of digital adversity.

MDR (MANAGED DETECTION AND RESPONSE)

DEFINITION

MDR is a managed service that combines technology and human expertise to provide organisations with threat-hunting, detection, and response capabilities. It goes beyond traditional security measures by actively seeking out threats and responding to them in real time.

MDR EXPLAINED

Imagine having a team of elite cybersecurity guards on watch 24/7, not just waiting for alarms but actively patrolling your digital estate, seeking out hidden threats. This is what MDR offers. It's like a cybersecurity SWAT team equipped with advanced tools and the expertise to detect subtle signs of compromise that might elude conventional defences. They don't just alert you to dangers; they dive into the fray, analysing and neutralising threats, often before they can harm. MDR represents a proactive stance in a landscape where reactive measures are no longer sufficient.

A MDR EXAMPLE

In the fall of 2022, a prominent online retailer experienced a sophisticated cyber attack aimed at stealing customer data. Thanks to their MDR service, the attack was detected early, contained, and neutralised with minimal impact. The MDR team quickly identified the attack's entry point, isolated affected systems, and eradicated the malware.

Post-incident, the retailer received a comprehensive report detailing the breach, the response actions taken, and recommendations for preventing future incidents. This incident demonstrated the MDR's pivotal role in modern cybersecurity strategies, providing peace of mind and a robust defence mechanism against increasingly sophisticated cyber threats.

MFA (MULTI-FACTOR AUTHENTICATION)

DEFINITION

MFA is a security system that uses multiple, independent authentication methods to verify a user's identity for logins or transactions.

MFA EXPLAINED

Imagine your digital identity is a vault, and MFA is the combination lock requiring multiple keys to open. It's an extra layer of defence, ensuring that even if one key (like a password) is compromised, unauthorised users can't access the vault without the additional keys (like a fingerprint or a unique code sent to your phone). MFA is about reinforcing security by combining something you know (like a password), something you have (like a smartphone), and something you are (like your fingerprint). This multi-layered approach significantly reduces the risk of unauthorised access, making MFA a cornerstone of modern digital security.

A MFA EXAMPLE

In 2022, a significant financial institution in the US heralded a new era of security for its customers by implementing mandatory MFA for all online banking services. This move directly responded to a surge in cyber fraud targeting the financial sector.

The rollout was more than a security upgrade; it was a commitment to safeguarding the financial well-being of millions. Customers embraced the change, recognising the value of the added security layer in protecting their hard-earned assets.

The initiative set a precedent in the industry, reinforcing that security is a shared responsibility in the digital age—a symphony of efforts from institutions and individuals alike to fortify the digital ramparts against the relentless tide of cyber threats.

MITM (MAN-IN-THE-MIDDLE) ATTACK

DEFINITION

An MITM attack is a form of eavesdropping in which the attacker secretly sits between two communicating parties and listens to, relays, and sometimes alters the information being passed without them realising it.

MITM EXPLAINED

Imagine a private conversation, only to discover someone secretly listening in and perhaps manipulating the exchanged messages. This is the essence of an MITM attack in the digital realm. The attacker intercepts the communication between the two people, becoming the invisible 'middleman.' Whether intercepting emails, tampering with transaction data, or stealing login credentials, MITM attacks exploit the trust between the communicating parties, turning confidential exchanges into opportunities for deception and theft.

A MITM EXAMPLE

In late 2023, a sophisticated MITM attack targeted a prominent European e-commerce platform during its peak sales season. Hackers infiltrated the communication between customers and the website, intercepting and altering transaction details.

The intrusion was subtle yet insidious, siphoning funds and sensitive customer data. But the platform's robust security measures, including end-to-end encryption and continuous monitoring, quickly identified and neutralised the threat.

This incident was more than a thwarted attack; it was a stark portrayal of the ingenuity of cyber adversaries and the critical importance of vigilance and advanced security measures in maintaining the sanctity of digital communication.

NAC (NETWORK ACCESS CONTROL)

DEFINITION

NAC is a security solution that enforces policy-based access control to network resources. It restricts the availability of network resources to endpoint devices based on their compliance with security policies.

NAC EXPLAINED

Imagine a club with a strict entry policy, where a bouncer checks each guest against a list of criteria before granting them access. NAC works similarly for network resources, serving as the digital bouncer for an organisation's network. It assesses devices trying to connect to the network, checking if they meet the set security standards—like up-to-date anti-virus protection or specific configurations. Devices that don't comply are denied access or placed in quarantine until they meet the necessary security requirements. NAC helps ensure that only secure, policy-compliant devices can access network resources, significantly reducing the risk of malware spread or data breaches.

A NAC EXAMPLE

A large university grappling with securing its network against threats introduced by countless student and faculty devices implemented an NAC solution in 2019. The NAC system was configured to verify that all devices met the university's security standards before allowing access to its network.

When an infected laptop attempted to connect, the NAC system immediately identified it as non-compliant. It restricted its network access, preventing a potential malware outbreak. This proactive approach safeguarded the university's digital resources and educated the community on the importance of maintaining device security, showcasing NAC's role in enforcing cybersecurity hygiene across diverse and dynamic environments.

NIST (NATIONAL INSTITUTE OF STANDARDS AND TECHNOLOGY)

DEFINITION

NIST is a US government agency that develops technology, metrics, and standards to drive innovation and economic competitiveness. These include comprehensive frameworks and guidelines for improving cybersecurity and privacy practices within organisations.

NIST EXPLAINED

Imagine a world-class team of scientists and experts dedicated to setting the gold standards for technology and security practices. NIST plays this role, especially in the realm of cybersecurity, offering a treasure trove of guidelines, frameworks, and best practices designed to help organisations protect their information and systems. From the NIST Cybersecurity Framework to standards for encryption, NIST's contributions are foundational to modern cybersecurity efforts, serving as both a beacon and a benchmark for organisations striving to enhance their security posture in a rapidly evolving digital landscape.

A NIST EXAMPLE

In response to rising cyber threats targeting the financial sector, a coalition of banks and financial institutions across the US adopted the NIST Cybersecurity Framework in 2016. This strategic move aimed to standardise their cybersecurity practices and strengthen their defences against cyber attacks.

The adoption process involved a comprehensive assessment of existing cybersecurity measures, alignment with NIST's guidelines, and implementation of recommended security controls. This collective effort significantly improved the sector's resilience against cyber threats. It fostered a culture of continuous improvement and collaboration in cybersecurity practices. The initiative highlighted NIST's pivotal role in shaping critical sectors' effective and adaptive cybersecurity strategies.

"51 ESSENTIAL CYBER TERMS EXPLAINED FOR LEADERS" REVIEW PAGE

"If your actions inspire others to dream more, learn more, do more and become more, you are a leader."
~ John Quincy Adams

We hope that you are finding the book useful. I suspect that there are many other leaders out there, who were like you used to be. Less experienced, needing answers, but not sure who or what to trust.

Most people do, in fact, judge a book by its cover (and its reviews). So here's my request to you as an amazing leader who I know is committed to helping others succeed.

Please help that leader by leaving this book a review.

It's remarkably hassle-free, it doesn't cost you anything, it will take about 60 seconds and your review really could help.

If you are **on audible** - hit the three dots in the top right of your device, click rate & review, then leave a few sentences about the book with a star rating.

If you are reading on **kindle, iPad or other tablet** - scroll to the bottom of the book, then swipe up and it will prompt a review for you.

If for some reason these are working for you, then go to Amazon and leave a review right **on the book's page**. Here's the link:

https://www.amazon.com/review/review-your-purchases/?asin=B0CXFQPNCH

If all fails, **scan this QR code**:

Thank you for doing that. It makes more of a difference to the next leader who may be considering whether to get this book

than you realize.

Right, let's get back to the main event. On with more of those essential cyber terms, definitions and explanations.

Thank you so much

Marco and Andrew

London, February 2024

Chapter 7

FROM O TO P

PAM (PRIVILEGED ACCESS MANAGEMENT)

DEFINITION

PAM is a set of cybersecurity strategies and technologies used to control, monitor, and secure access to an organisation's critical information and resources by privileged users, such as administrators and executives.

PAM EXPLAINED

Consider PAM as the vault within a bank, where only a select few can access the most valuable assets. In the digital domain, PAM protects an organisation's most sensitive systems and data by ensuring that only authorised individuals with privileged access can interact with them. This is crucial because privileged accounts are prime targets for attackers, given their high level of access. PAM restricts this access based on necessity and keeps detailed records of who accesses what and when adding a layer of accountability and security vital for protecting an organisation's crown jewels.

A PAM EXAMPLE

In 2023, a leading global corporation faced a potentially catastrophic data breach when attackers targeted privileged accounts. Thanks to its robust PAM system, the company could quickly identify unusual access patterns and intervene before sensitive data was compromised.

The PAM system's real-time monitoring and alerting capabilities enabled the security team to revoke the compromised credentials and limit the breach's scope. This incident underscored the importance of PAM in safeguarding against the exploitation of privileged access, reinforcing the corporation's commitment to a security-first approach in protecting its digital assets and maintaining stakeholder trust.

PATCH

DEFINITION

A patch is an update that incorporates changes, fixes, or improvements to a computer program or its supporting data. It often involves fixing security vulnerabilities and other bugs.

PATCH EXPLAINED

Consider a patch as the digital world's version of a band-aid, but smarter. Just as a Band-Aid covers a wound to help it heal, a software patch covers vulnerabilities in a program, protecting it from cyber threats. These patches can fix bugs, add new features, or close security loopholes. As cyber threats evolve, patches are released regularly by software vendors to ensure users stay one step ahead of potential attackers. Refraining from paying attention to these updates is akin to leaving your digital doors unlocked, inviting trouble.

A PATCH EXAMPLE

2023, a critical vulnerability was discovered in a widely used database software, affecting thousands of organisations worldwide, including a large Australian bank. The vulnerability, if exploited, could give attackers unrestricted access to sensitive data.

The software vendor acted swiftly, releasing a patch to address the flaw. With its robust cybersecurity protocols, the Australian bank promptly applied the patch network-wide. This proactive response averted what could have been a catastrophic data breach, underscoring the paramount importance of regular software maintenance and the vigilant application of patches in safeguarding digital assets.

PHISHING

DEFINITION

Phishing is a deliberate and fraudulent attempt to obtain sensitive information such as usernames, passwords, and credit card details, usually in sophisticated emails that look like they come from the actual sender,

PHISHING EXPLAINED

Imagine a fisherman casting his baited hook into the lake, waiting for an unsuspecting fish to bite. Phishing operates similarly in the digital sea. Cybercriminals cast deceptive emails or messages, mimicking legitimate sources like banks or service providers, luring individuals into revealing personal information. These messages often create a sense of fear, prompting hasty actions. Phishing preys on human trust and curiosity, turning ordinary interactions into potential traps, making it one of the most prevalent and pernicious threats in the cyber world.

A PHISHING EXAMPLE

In a high-stakes incident in 2022, a European government agency became the target of a sophisticated phishing campaign. Employees received emails from the IT department urging them to update their passwords due to a security breach.

The emails were convincing, complete with official logos and persuasive language. However, a vigilant employee reported a slight discrepancy in the email address. The agency's quick response and employee cybersecurity training averted a potential disaster, safeguarding sensitive government data and reinforcing the critical role of awareness and vigilance in combating the ever-present phishing threat.

PII (PERSONALLY IDENTIFIABLE INFORMATION)

DEFINITION

PII refers to information that can be used alone or in conjunction with other information to identify, contact, or locate a single person or to identify an individual in context. Protecting PII is essential for personal privacy and data security.

PII EXPLAINED

Imagine every piece of data about you—your name, address, email, phone number—being keys to your digital identity. These keys can unlock doors to fraud, identity theft, and privacy violations in the wrong hands. PII encompasses these keys, making its protection a cornerstone of individual privacy and organisational data security strategies. In a world where data is constantly collected and analysed, ensuring the confidentiality and integrity of PII is not just a legal obligation for organisations but a fundamental aspect of trust and safety in the digital age.

A PII EXAMPLE

In 2022, a significant healthcare provider implemented cutting-edge data protection measures to safeguard its patients' PII. This initiative was critically tested when a sophisticated phishing attack aimed at extracting patient PII was identified.

The healthcare provider's advanced encryption and access control measures ensured the attackers could not obtain any usable PII. Furthermore, the incident prompted a comprehensive review of data security practices. This led to enhanced staff training on identifying and preventing phishing attempts. This proactive stance protected patients' sensitive information and reinforced the healthcare provider's reputation as a trusted guardian of personal privacy.

PKI (PUBLIC KEY INFRASTRUCTURE)

DEFINITION

PKI is a framework of policies, roles, hardware, software, and procedures to create, manage, distribute, use, store, and revoke digital certificates and manage public-key encryption. It establishes trust within an environment by verifying entities' identities and encrypting data transmission.

PKI EXPLAINED

Imagine sending a sealed, secret message in a bottle across a vast ocean, where anyone might intercept it. PKI is like a sophisticated cryptographic system that ensures only the intended recipient can open and read your message, thanks to a pair of public and private keys. It's the backbone of secure digital communication, enabling activities like secure emails, confidential online transactions, and the signing of digital documents. By authenticating the identities and encrypting the data exchanged, PKI plays a crucial role in establishing a secure and trustworthy digital world.

EXAMPLE

In 2023, a large international bank faced a challenge: ensuring the authenticity and security of its digital transactions worldwide. The bank implemented a robust PKI system, issuing digital certificates to clients and devices, establishing a secure environment for online banking.

This implementation proved its worth when an attempt was made to breach the bank's transaction system using forged credentials. The PKI framework successfully identified and blocked unauthorised access, ensuring the integrity and security of millions of transactions. The bank's commitment to using PKI protected its customers' assets. It reinforced the critical importance of digital trust in the financial sector.

Chapter 8

FROM Q TO S

RANSOMWARE

DEFINITION

Ransomware is malicious software designed to block access to a computer system or data until a payment is made. Modern versions often exfiltrate information from the attacked computer system for further revenue opportunities.

RANSOMWARE EXPLAINED

Envision walking into your home to find your valuables locked away, with a ransom note demanding payment for their return. This is what ransomware does in the digital domain. It holds your data, or even your entire system, hostage, demanding payment for its release. The attack can paralyse individuals and organisations, leading to a painful dilemma:

pay the ransom and fund criminal activities, or lose precious data and face potential operational havoc. Ransomware is a formidable weapon in the cyber criminal's arsenal, leveraging the power of encryption for extortion.

A RANSOMWARE EXAMPLE

In a dramatic showdown in early 2023, a prominent US hospital chain was hit by a devastating ransomware attack. Critical patient data and healthcare systems were encrypted, disrupting services and risking lives.

The attackers demanded a hefty ransom, but the hospital stood firm, refusing to negotiate with criminals. Instead, they relied on their robust backup systems and comprehensive incident response plan. The recovery was arduous but successful, highlighting the importance of preparedness and resilience in the face of the growing threat of ransomware attacks in the healthcare industry.

ROOTKIT

DEFINITION

A rootkit is software used by cybercriminals to gain control over a target computer or network. Rootkits can sometimes appear as a single piece of software but are often made up of a collection of tools that allow hackers administrator-level control over the target device.

ROOTKIT EXPLAINED

Imagine a spy infiltrating a government building, hiding and eavesdropping confidential meetings undetected. A rootkit does something similar in the digital world. It's a stealthy type of malware that burrows deep into a system, hiding its presence and the presence of other malicious software. Once installed, it can give attackers control over your system, spy on your actions, and steal sensitive data. Rootkits are particularly insidious because they can be hard to detect, allowing them to operate unnoticed for long periods.

A ROOTKIT EXAMPLE

In late 2023, a major European telecommunication company discovered a sophisticated rootkit in its core network infrastructure. The rootkit had been quietly siphoning sensitive data and compromising network integrity for months.

The discovery shocked the system, prompting an immediate and comprehensive security overhaul. The company's swift response and transparent communication with customers and authorities set a new standard in handling such stealthy and sophisticated threats. This incident was a stark reminder of the insidious nature of rootkits and the constant vigilance required to protect digital infrastructure in the high-stakes world of telecommunications.

SOAR (SECURITY ORCHESTRATION, AUTOMATION, AND RESPONSE)

DEFINITION

SOAR refers to technologies that enable organisations to collect data about security threats from multiple sources and respond to low-level security events without human intervention, using automated processes.

SOAR EXPLAINED

Imagine a symphony orchestra where each musician plays their part, led by a conductor, to create a harmonious performance. SOAR does something similar for cybersecurity. It orchestrates various security tools and systems, automates the response to routine threats, and enables a coordinated response to more complex incidents. This not only speeds up an organisation's ability to respond to attacks but also frees up security teams to focus on more strategic tasks, enhancing overall security posture with efficiency and precision.

A SOAR EXAMPLE

In 2020, a multinational corporation faced a relentless wave of phishing attacks. Implementing a SOAR solution transformed its response capabilities. The SOAR system automatically identified and quarantined phishing emails, significantly reducing the threat's impact.

This automation allowed the security team to concentrate on analysing the attack patterns, leading to the identification of the attackers' command and control servers. The swift, orchestrated response mitigated the immediate threat. It provided actionable intelligence for preventing future attacks, demonstrating the power of SOAR in enhancing cybersecurity resilience.

SOC (SECURITY OPERATIONS CENTRE)

DEFINITION

A SOC is a centralised unit that deals with security issues on an organisational and technical level. It comprises a team with the necessary tools and technologies to monitor, analyse, and protect an organisation from cyber threats.

SOC EXPLAINED

Think of a SOC as the high-tech command centre for a company's cybersecurity efforts. Within this centre, a dedicated team of security experts works around the clock, using state-of-the-art technology to monitor the organisation's networks for any signs of a security breach. They're the digital-first responders, ready to detect, analyse, and respond to cyber incidents and threats. The SOC is critical in minimising the impact of attacks by ensuring rapid detection and response, akin to a well-coordinated defence force safeguarding the digital fortress of an organisation.

A SOC EXAMPLE

In 2018, a tech conglomerate was targeted by a complex cyber espionage campaign. Thanks to the vigilance of its SOC, the attack was detected early. The SOC team quickly acted, isolating the affected systems and using forensic tools to analyse the attack's nature and origin.

Their rapid response prevented the exfiltration of sensitive data and minimised downtime. Post-attack, the SOC's thorough investigation provided insights that strengthened the company's cyber defences, showcasing the indispensable role of SOCs in defending against and learning from cyber threats.

SPEAR PHISHING

DEFINITION

Spear phishing is an email-spoofing attack that targets a specific organisation, group or individual seeking unauthorised access to confidential data. Unlike phishing attacks, spear phishing attackers often gather and use personal information about their target to increase their probability of success.

SPEAR PHISHING EXPLAINED

Spear phishing is the digital world's sniper – precise, targeted, and dangerous. It's like phishing but more personalised and deceptive. Attackers do their homework, collecting information about their target to craft convincing messages, often impersonating colleagues, friends, or trusted authorities. The aim is to trick the recipient into divulging sensitive information or clicking on malicious links. The personal nature of spear phishing makes it highly effective and dangerous, turning familiarity and trust into weapons against the unwary.

A SPEAR PHISHING EXAMPLE

In a riveting case in 2023, a top executive at a prominent German manufacturing company fell victim to a spear-phishing attack. The attacker, posing as a trusted supplier, sent an email with a seemingly legitimate invoice. The email, however, contained a malicious link that, once clicked, granted the attacker access to the company's confidential financial data.

The precision and personalisation of the attack caught everyone off guard. However, the company's robust cybersecurity training and quick incident response mechanisms prevented further damage. The incident was a critical lesson for the company and the industry, highlighting the evolving sophistication of cyber threats and the imperative of continuous vigilance and education in cybersecurity practices.

Chapter 9

FROM MORE S TO T

SQL INJECTION

DEFINITION

Structured query language (SQL) is a standard language for database creation and manipulation. Therefore, SQL Injection is a technique where attackers insert malicious SQL code into data-driven applications via input fields to manipulate or access the database.

SQL INJECTION EXPLAINED

Imagine a bank vault with a voice recognition system that opens the door if you say the correct password. What if someone finds a way to trick the system into opening the door by embedding a command in their request? That's akin to an SQL Injection in the digital realm. Hackers inject malicious SQL commands into data fields of applications (like login forms) to manipulate the database, often to view, steal, or delete data they shouldn't have access to. It's a cunning exploit that uses insufficiently protected application code, turning regular user input into a back-door key to sensitive data.

SQL INJECTION EXAMPLE

In 2022, a renowned British e-commerce platform fell victim to a sophisticated SQL Injection attack. The attackers cleverly embedded malicious SQL code into the website's search box, granting them unauthorised access to the company's customer database. Personal details, including credit card information, were compromised.

The attack was a digital heist, cunning in execution and devastating in impact. However, the company's swift action, transparent communication, and subsequent security enhancements turned the crisis into a rallying point. It sparked an industry-wide initiative to fortify defences against SQL Injection, emphasising the critical need for stringent input validation and constant vigilance in an ever-evolving threat landscape.

SSL/TLS (SECURE SOCKETS LAYER/ TRANSPORT LAYER SECURITY)

DEFINITION

SSL and TLS are cryptographic protocols designed to secure communications over a computer network. They encrypt data transmitted between a user's browser and a web server, ensuring the confidentiality and integrity of the information exchanged.

SSL/TLS EXPLAINED

Imagine sending a sealed, coded letter in a world where messages are often intercepted and read. SSL/TLS does that for digital communications. Visiting a website with SSL/TLS is like having an exclusive, secure channel between your browser and the server. Your data – passwords, credit card numbers, or personal messages – travels encrypted, shielded from prying eyes. Even if intercepted, the data remains unreadable to anyone without the specific key. In an age where data breaches are rampant, SSL/TLS is responsible for privacy and security in digital communications.

A SSL/TLS EXAMPLE

In 2023, amidst rising concerns over data interception, a major European bank took a significant step by upgrading its online banking platform to the latest TLS standards. The move was a technical upgrade and a commitment to customer trust and data security.

As customers engaged in transactions, the enhanced encryption turned their sensitive financial data into indecipherable code, impervious to lurking cyber threats. The bank's initiative set a benchmark, highlighting the pivotal role of robust encryption standards like SSL/TLS in securing digital transactions and fostering an environment of trust and safety in the financial industry.

SSO (SINGLE SIGN-ON)

DEFINITION

SSO is an authentication process that allows a user to access multiple applications or systems with one set of login credentials. It enhances user convenience and improves security by reducing the number of passwords users must manage.

SSO EXPLAINED

Think of SSO as a master key that unlocks multiple doors. Instead of juggling a heavy keyring, you have one key that grants access to everything you need. In the digital realm, SSO streamlines the login process, allowing users to navigate seamlessly between services without repeatedly entering credentials. This simplifies the user experience and strengthens security by minimising the risk of password fatigue and the subsequent use of weak passwords. SSO represents a balance between convenience and security in the access management landscape.

A SSO EXAMPLE

In 2021, a significant healthcare network implemented SSO to streamline staff and patients' access to its various digital services. The move significantly improved operational efficiency, reducing login times and password-related help desk calls.

When a cybersecurity audit revealed a potential vulnerability in the network's previous authentication system, the SSO solution's centralised management made it easy to address and secure the vulnerability. This proactive approach not only safeguarded sensitive health data but also reinforced the network's reputation for patient care and data protection, illustrating the strategic value of SSO in modern IT environments.

TROJAN HORSE

DEFINITION

A Trojan horse, or Trojan, is a type of malware that disguises itself as legitimate software. Users are tricked into loading and executing the Trojan on their systems, which can lead to data theft, damage, or disruptive behaviour.

TROJAN HORSE EXPLAINED

Imagine receiving a gift that, unbeknown to you, contains a hidden spy. That's the digital equivalent of a Trojan horse. It masquerades as a harmless app or software, enticing users to download or open it. Once activated, it can unleash chaos, steal data, create back doors for future attacks, or even hijack system resources. Unlike viruses, Trojans don't replicate themselves but rely on the guise of legitimacy to infiltrate and carry out their malicious intents. The deceitful nature of Trojans makes them a formidable tool in the cyber criminal's arsenal.

TROJAN HORSE EXAMPLE

In a high-profile incident in 2023, a prominent American media company was blindsided by a Trojan disguised as a routine software update. The Trojan silently infiltrated the company's network, granting attackers unprecedented access to confidential content, proprietary data, and sensitive employee information.

The breach was a digital wildfire, spreading rapidly and covertly. However, the company's robust incident response strategy stemmed the tide, isolating the Trojan and mitigating its impact. The aftermath was a period of introspection and reinforcement as the company and the wider industry grappled with the stark reminder of the persistent and deceptive threat posed by Trojans in the digital era.

TTP (TACTICS, TECHNIQUES, AND PROCEDURES)

DEFINITION

TTPs are the patterns of activities or methods associated with a specific threat actor or group of actors. Understanding an attacker's TTPs helps cybersecurity professionals more effectively anticipate and mitigate potential threats. Advanced Persistent Threats are identified and categorised by the TTPs they employ.

TTP EXPLAINED

Imagine studying the playbook of an opposing sports team; knowing their strategies gives you an advantage. TTPs in cybersecurity involve understanding how adversaries operate—their tactics (what they do), techniques (how they do it), and procedures (the tools they use). By analysing TTPs, security teams can better predict and prepare for potential attacks, tailoring their defences to counter specific threats. It's a critical aspect of cybersecurity intelligence, turning abstract data about past attacks into actionable insights for future defence.

A TTP EXAMPLE

In 2017, after noticing a pattern of security breaches targeting similar organisations, a cybersecurity firm conducted an in-depth analysis of the incidents. They identified specific TTPs consistent across the attacks linked to a well-known cyber-criminal group.

With this knowledge, the firm developed and deployed targeted defence strategies for its clients, successfully thwarting attempted breaches. The firm's ability to decode and act on the attackers' TTPs protected its clients. It contributed valuable intelligence to the broader cybersecurity community, highlighting the strategic importance of understanding TTPs in combating cyber threats.

Chapter 10

FROM U TO Z

UBA (USER BEHAVIOUR ANALYTICS)

DEFINITION

UBA is a cybersecurity process that uses analytics to identify abnormal behaviour or activities by monitoring and analysing user interactions with applications and systems. It helps detect insider threats, compromised accounts, and other security risks based on deviations from standard behaviour patterns.

UBA EXPLAINED

Imagine having a keenly observant friend at a party who notices when someone starts acting out of character, suggesting they might need help. UBA acts similarly within an organisation's network, constantly monitoring how users interact with systems and spotting unusual behaviour that could indicate a security issue. Whether it's a user accessing files they usually wouldn't or logging in at odd hours, UBA helps pinpoint potential security risks by flagging these anomalies for further investigation. It's an essential tool in the modern security toolkit, offering insights into actions that may go unnoticed.

AN UBA EXAMPLE

In 2019, a global financial institution employed UBA to enhance its security posture amid rising concerns over insider threats. The system flagged unusual activity from a high-ranking executive's account—access to sensitive files at an odd hour.

Upon investigation, it was determined that the executive's credentials had been compromised. The quick detection allowed the institution to immediately secure the account and prevent a potentially devastating data leak. This incident underscored the value of UBA in detecting and responding to sophisticated threats, demonstrating its efficacy in safeguarding against external and internal security challenges.

VPN (VIRTUAL PRIVATE NETWORK)

DEFINITION

A VPN extends a private network across a public network, allowing users to send and receive data across shared or more public networks as if their computers or devices were connected directly to the private network. Encrypting the data in transit enhances privacy and security.

VPN EXPLAINED

Imagine a secure, private tunnel through the chaos of a crowded, public space. A VPN provides such a tunnel in the digital world. It lets you connect to the Internet privately and securely, shielding your data from eavesdroppers and hackers. Whether working remotely, accessing sensitive information, or just seeking privacy, a VPN encrypts your connection, making your online activities unreadable to outsiders. In an era of heightened surveillance and data breaches, a VPN is essential for preserving the confidentiality and integrity of digital communications.

A VPN EXAMPLE

In 2023, amidst growing concerns over remote work security, a multinational corporation headquartered in Canada implemented a mandatory VPN policy for all employees accessing the corporate network remotely. The decision was more than a security protocol; it was a strategic move to safeguard corporate data in the face of escalating cyber threats.

The VPN encrypted employee communications, rendering data transfers secure and invisible to potential intruders. The company's commitment to VPN usage exemplified a proactive stance on digital security, setting a precedent for remote work protocols and reinforcing the significance of VPNs in building a resilient, secure remote work infrastructure.

ZERO-DAY EXPLOIT

DEFINITION

"Zero-day" is a broad term that describes recently discovered security vulnerabilities that hackers can use to attack systems. The term "zero-day" refers to the fact that the vendor or developer has only just learned of the flaw – which means they have "zero days" to fix it. A zero-day attack takes place when hackers exploit the flaw before developers have a chance to address it.

ZERO-DAY EXPLOIT EXPLAINED

Imagine a thief discovering a secret entrance to a bank vault before the bank even knows it exists. That's the essence of a zero-day exploit in the cyber realm. It's an attack on a software flaw the vendor is unaware of and has had no time to fix. Attackers highly prize these vulnerabilities because they can be exploited to gain unauthorised access, steal data, or cause disruption before a defence can be developed. The race against time to discover and patch these vulnerabilities is critical to cyber-security.

A ZERO-DAY EXPLOIT EXAMPLE

In a dramatic cyber-security event in 2023, a leading software company faced a formidable challenge when a zero-day exploit in its widely used office suite was disclosed. The exploit allowed attackers to execute code remotely, compromising user data and system integrity.

Upon discovering the exploit, the company acted with precision and urgency. It released an emergency patch and communicated transparently with its user base, emphasising the importance of immediate updates. The prompt response mitigated the potential damage and highlighted the company's commitment to user security and the relentless battle against the invisible yet ever-present threat of zero-day exploits in the digital world.

.

CONCLUSION

As we draw this to a close, we should remember that the topic of cybersecurity is constantly expanding and becoming yet more sophisticated, demanding not only our attention but also our active engagement.

This book, *"51 Essential Cyber Terms Explained for Leaders"* was conceived as a bridge between the often challenging world of cyber experts and the strategic role of leadership. We've simplified complex terms and concepts, demystifying them and bringing them to life. Hopefully, what might once have seemed like a foreign dialect now feels more transparent, easier to understand, and to use with increased fluency.

This transformation happens not merely because of the accumulation of knowledge but in applying that knowledge. The definitions, explanations, and case studies presented here are more than academic exercises; they are tools for action. By integrating these concepts into your decision-making processes, you enhance your personal leadership toolkit and fortify your organization against the multifaceted threats of the digital age.

Reflecting on the content covered, it's evident that cybersecurity is not a concern that can be delegated away or side-lined. It is a central aspect of modern business strategy, intertwined with every facet of our operations and objectives. The clarity with which you now understand terms like "endpoint security," "ransomware," and "spear phishing" equips you to ask more pointed questions, make more informed decisions, and foster a culture of awareness and resilience within your team.

This newfound fluency serves a dual purpose. First, it bridges the gap between you and your technical teams, enabling more effective communication and collaboration. No longer lost in translation, your discussions can dive deeper, unlocking innovative solutions and strategies previously obscured by misunderstandings or misinterpretations. Second, it positions you as a leader who is prepared to face current challenges and anticipate future ones. Such foresight is invaluable in an era where digital advancements occur at breakneck speed.

Moreover, the benefits of this increased confidence extend beyond your organization's confines. Mastering these critical cyber concepts raises the bar for cybersecurity awareness and preparedness in your industry and community. This collective elevation of knowledge and capability is our best defense against the cyber threats that loom large over our interconnected world.

It's also worth noting that cybersecurity is perpetually evolving, shaped by the relentless emergence of new technologies, threats, and opportunities.

While this book provides a solid foundation, the pursuit of cyber fluency is continuous. Please remain curious, stay abreast of developments in the field, and reflect on how they might impact your leadership and your organization.

Resources for ongoing learning include cybersecurity news platforms, industry reports, and professional networks—each offering fresh insights and perspectives to enrich your understanding.

In closing, this book has served as a guide and a catalyst, inspiring you to embrace the complexities of cybersecurity with confidence and curiosity. The shift from uncertainty to understanding, from apprehension to action, marks a significant leap in your leadership journey. By demystifying the jargon and concepts of the cyber world, you've gained both knowledge and a strategic advantage. This advantage will serve you, your team, and your organization in countless ways.

Remember, the significance of cybersecurity extends far beyond protecting data or systems; it's about safeguarding the trust placed in us by our customers, employees, and stakeholders. This trust is the foundation upon which our businesses are built, and our reputations are maintained. As leaders, we are responsible for upholding this trust, ensuring that our actions and decisions reflect a deep commitment to the security and well-being of all those we serve.

In this spirit, I thank you for joining me in this critical exploration. The following steps you take, armed with the insights and understanding you've gained, will fortify your leadership and contribute to a safer, more secure future for everyone in the digital realm. Let us move forward with the resolve to apply our knowledge diligently, lead with wisdom and foresight, and make a lasting impact in the ever-evolving world of cybersecurity.

Marco Ryan And Andrew Fitzmaurice

London , February 2024

ABOUT THE AUTHORS

Marco is a renowned expert in digital transformation, data management, Artificial Intelligence, and Cybersecurity.

With a comprehensive understanding of the evolving digital landscape, gained through years of Operational experience Marco brings a wealth of experience and expertise to guide readers through the world of Artificial Intelligence, Cybersecurity and Digital Transformation.

As the Cyber Leader in Residence at Lancaster University Management School and a former Global Chief Digital Officer and Senior Vice President Digital for BP, Marco is committed to empowering readers with the knowledge and skills necessary to navigate the digital future.

He has extensive public speaking experience, including Ted talks, regularly delivering Keynotes at major conferences or for companies as part of workshops or off-sites.

To discuss options for working with Marco, whether for group or individual coaching or to explore having him deliver a keynote address, please use the QR code or click the link to his website.

https://marcoryan.com

Andrew is CEO of Templar Executives, an international, award winning Cyber Security advisory company; he leads an expert management team delivering world-class Cyber Security consultancy services and solutions. Andrew specialises in government and commercial sector board-level engagements and transformational change programmes to enhance business performance. He has also established the Templar Cyber Academy whose range of courses and training are uniquely certified by NCSC.

A thought leader and accomplished speaker and author, Andrew is regularly invited to contribute and speak on Cyber Security, Information Assurance and Governance topics. He in partnership with Lancaster University has led the development of a Cyber Executive MBA aimed at senior executives. He is strategic advisor to the Global Capacity

Building Centre at the Oxford Martin School at Oxford University. He has also taken part in the FCO Commonwealth Cyber Security Programme as a mentor to Ministers from the Commonwealth Countries.

Andrew's background includes 18 years in the military specialising in air command and control. He has worked in the Cabinet Office where he set up and ran the Office of the Government Senior Information Risk Owner (OGSIRO). Andrew has also been closely involved in authoring key publications and policies including: The Data Handling Review (Hannigan Report); The IA Diagnostic Methodology; the Ministry of Defence Information Assurance Strategy and the UK's National Information Assurance/Cyber Security strategies.

https://templarexecs.com

RESOURCES

Admin. (2023, August 18). *What is Botnet* - @starlinenews. com. starlinenews.com. https://starlinenews.com/botnet/

User. (2022, October 11). *malware – Scarab* Net. https:// scarabnet.org/?p=415

HealPay. (2023, August 21). *The role of Multi-Factor Authentication in strong data security*. HealPay Payment Software Blog. https://blog.healpay.com/blog/multi-factor-authentication/

Most common threats of public Wi-Fi. (2019, August 5). The TNS Group. https://thetnsgroup.com/managed-service-provider/tns-managed-service-provider-threats-of-public-wifi/

Sekar, R. (2023, May 1). *Hostname verification: Preventing Man-in-the-Middle attacks. DEV Community.* https://practicaldev-herokuapp-com.global.ssl.fastly.net/rathishsekar/hostname-verification-preventing-man-in-the-middle-attacks-3nfi

Ransomware | UA Information Security. (n.d.). https:// security.arizona.edu/content/ransomware

Pritz, A. (n.d.). *Deep Sea Phishing: A taxonomy for email cyber threats* – Reveal risk – Cybersecurity Consulting and Services. https://www.revealrisk.com/hello-world/

Interactive, S. (2022, January 21). *Virtual Private Network (VPN) definition* - Brightwhiz.com. Brightwhiz.com. https://brightwhiz.com/glossary/virtual-private-network/

Lobos, C. (2023, May 9). *Companies turn to BYOD policies and IT expense management solutions to increase productivity and security.* https://blog.asignet.com/companies-turn-to-byod-policies-and-it-expense-management-solutions-to-increase-productivity-and-security

Shadow IT Discovery Methods | RESMO. (n.d.). https://www.resmo.com/blog/shadow-it-discovery-methods

Arnet Technologies, Inc. (2023, July 7). *Arm Your Business with an Array of Cybersecurity Tools* | Blog. https://www.arnettechnologies.com/arm-your-business-with-an-array-of-cybersecurity-tools/

TheCconnects, T. (2023, June 19). *Complete guide to operational technology* - TheCconnects. TheCconnects. https://thecconnects.com/complete-guide-to-operational-technology/

ISO 27000 - CIO Wiki. (n.d.). https://cio-wiki.org/index.php?title=ISO_27000&oldid=7322

Colorado Small Business Development Center Network. (2023, December 5). *The Gist on the Nist.* https://clients.coloradosbdc.org/workshop.aspx?ekey=20430279

Printed in Great Britain
by Amazon

44347674R00056